Think about it...
Journeys

Harry Cory Wright

W
FRANKLIN WATTS
LONDON • SYDNEY

Where do you think these
geese may be going?

What would you pack for a long journey?

What would it be like to fly above
the clouds like this?

What would it be like to be inside this aeroplane?
What do you think some of these dials are for?

How might you get to this house?

What would this be like?

Why has this man stopped here?

Can you make up a story
that starts at this station?

What do you think it
would be like to go
camping here?

What might people do when travelling by train?

Imagine you were here.
What would be going through your head?

How would you like to
travel up this river?

Who would you go with?

Where would you like to go
on this road?

Who do you think might be travelling on this train?

Where might this boy be going?

How would you
feel if you were
standing here?

What sounds might
you hear?

Journeys

What is travelling all about? Why do we go to different places and what's it like to get there? Travelling is about going away at weekends or in the holidays, but it's also about little trips to the shops, running down a hill and all the journeys in our imagination. What's it like to travel up a river, to go on a boat on the sea or to camp in a field? In this book we ask questions that can start some rich discussions about what it is like to go on a journey.

A framework for exploration

'What's going on in this picture?' is a question that is asked by children and adults alike whenever presented with a photograph. Usually the answer is in the caption. But what if we ask questions rather than provide answers? What if there is no right answer? The photographs in this book are intended to be starting points for children to explore ideas. Remember, there are no rules here, let alone any right answers – children can take a simple idea and run with it as far as they wish.

The teacher or parent should use his or her judgement to decide the appropriate depth of discussion according to the abilities of the child. Some children may describe only what they see in the picture in clear sentences. Other children should be able to extend the themes and offer in-depth explanations and opinions. Ideas for expanding each theme are listed below in 'Talk about', but you may also ask some general questions on the theme of journeys such as: what would this journey feel like?

Where do you think these geese may be going? (pages 2–3)
These are pink-footed geese that come to Norfolk where I live for the winter. They arrive in their tens of thousands in the autumn from their breeding grounds up by the Arctic Circle. Here they are flying against a stiff breeze on a sunny day, probably on their way to feed on fields inland from where they roost by the sea overnight.
Talk about: • why birds migrate and how this links with the seasons • what it might feel like to fly like a bird • what the world would look like from a bird's eye view.

What would you pack for a long journey? (pages 4–5)
This is a case packed by a friend of one of my daughters. There was a reason of course for each thing she packed and much thought went into it all.

Talk about: • what you would take on holiday • what might you have to leave behind • if you could only take one thing what it would be • how much it would depend on where you were going • whether packing is part of a journey.

What would it be like to fly above the clouds like this? (page 6)
This was on a flight to Europe. The clouds looked so quiet and gentle and the evening light picks out their shape nicely.
Talk about: • what might be below the clouds • why it would be sunny above the clouds even if the weather was wet at ground level • what else you might see up there • what you would be feeling if you were in that aeroplane • the atmosphere in the aircraft.

What would it be like to be inside this aeroplane? What do you think some of these dials are for? (page 7)
This is the flight deck of Concorde. I photographed it just for this book. It was quite cramped in the cockpit.
Talk about: • what Concorde is • what kind of trips Concorde may have done • the people who may have flown in it • what sounds might you have heard as it takes off • if it would have been fun to fly such an aircraft • where you would want to visit.

How might you get to this house? What would it be like when you got there? (pages 8–9)

This is on a little island in the Outer Hebrides in Scotland. It is very remote and nobody lives there now. In good weather it is a glorious place but in bad weather it's very lonely indeed. You can get there only by boat or helicopter.

Talk about: • other vessels you might see passing by • why people would live on islands like this • why people go on holiday to 'get away from it all' sometimes.

What would this be like? (pages 10–11)

This is my son Joe on a fishing trip off the south coast of England. It was warm and sunny and we caught many different kinds of fish. There were about 10 of us on the boat and we had a great time.

Talk about: • who you might like to do this with and what it might be like when you got home • what travelling on the sea is like – in good and bad weather • what kind of day trips they would like to go on • how many children have sailed on the sea – and their likes and dislikes of their experiences.

Why has this man stopped here? (pages 12–13)

This is a bridge across a canal in Paris. It was a lovely breezy, warm day and the man stopped to look at the view for a few minutes.

Talk about: • where he might have been going • why he was not in a hurry • what he might be looking at • where they would like to stroll.

Can you make up a story that starts at this station? (pages 14–15)

This is the Gard du Nord in Paris. It was very busy with lots of people leaving and arriving by train. The trains were coming from all over the north of France, with some people looking like commuters, but otherwise it was difficult to tell what their journey was about. Some people had lots of baggage, while others had very little.

Talk about: • whether busy stations are exciting or overwhelming • favourite stations • other busy places • noises they might hear in stations.

What do you think it would be like to go camping here? (pages 16–17)

This is my family asleep one summer morning when we were camping in a field. It was a very hot evening but with some mist rising from the river amongst the trees. We were travelling around the British Isles while I was working on a book about the landscape of the country. The children had a good time, but there were times when it wasn't easy. When do you think these might have been?

Talk about: • camping trips they have been on • what's good/bad about camping • different types of camping, such as tents, caravans, chalets – pros and cons of each/personal experiences.

What might people do when travelling by train? (page 18)

Here my daughter is going through her bag of things she brought for the journey.

Talk about: • what people take on journeys • why we take so much sometimes • what it would be like to take nothing and just look out of the window • things you may daydream about when you look out of a train window.

Imagine you were here. What would be going through your head? (page 19)

These people were travelling through Paris on a warm evening. They were smiling and looked very happy. Why might that be?

Talk about: • what it may feel like to drive a moped and be on the back of one • unusual ways to travel • keeping safe when travelling on bikes, especially motorbikes or mopeds.

How would you like to travel up this river? Who would you go with? (pages 20–21)
This is the River Trent early one morning. I love rivers at this time of day because there are no people about, just wildlife. It is like travelling in a quiet and gentle dream. I am always keen on landscape pictures that are on the one hand very strong and real but are also full of something 'other-worldly'.
Talk about: • why this picture has a dream-like quality • what travelling in dreams is like • what travelling in the boat would be like.

Where would you like to go on this road? (pages 22–23)

This road leads down to the sea in County Cork, Ireland. In bad weather it is an awesome place with the wind and rain coming right off the Atlantic Ocean. This picture has always felt very robust to me – like the road is a good thing, as much as a road can be. It's a road you would like to take just to see where it went.
Talk about: • where you think the road leads to • why some people might enjoy driving on such a road • the dangers of roads • keeping safe near roads.

Who do you think might be travelling on this train? (pages 24–25)
This train is travelling along an embankment through the Fens in the East of England. It was going very speedily and made a 'whooshing' noise as it went past. Afterwards we went up to the level crossing and watched other trains passing.
Talk about: • train use at different times of day and during the week or the weekend • how it feels when a train whooshes past you • what are the most exciting ways to travel • how we might travel in the future.

Where might this boy be going? (pages 26–27)
This boy was running downhill and nearly fell over just after I took the picture. It was in the afternoon and a few of us were playing about in a park above the city.
Talk about: • where he could be going • whether he may be chasing his friends or being chased • where he went after this • why we run to places sometimes.

How would you feel if you were standing here? What sounds might you hear? (pages 28–29)

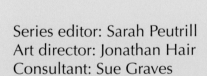

This is a train station in France. People would stop for what would seem all sorts of reasons; to look at maps, have a drink, wait for friends. Everyone was moving in different directions.
Talk about: • what busy places feel like • how it feels to be in a hurry – perhaps to be late for something.

First published in 2009
by Franklin Watts

Copyright © Harry Cory Wright 2009

Franklin Watts
338 Euston Road
London NW1 3BH

Franklin Watts Australia
Level 17/207 Kent Street
Sydney, NSW 2000

Series editor: Sarah Peutrill
Art director: Jonathan Hair
Consultant: Sue Graves

Dewey number: 388

ISBN 978 0 7496 8849 3

Printed in China

Franklin Watts is a division of Hachette Children's Books, an Hachette UK company.

www.hachette.co.uk